Biking
An Outdoor Adventure Handbook

Biking

An Outdoor Adventure Handbook

Hugh McManners

DORLING KINDERSLEY
London • New York • Stuttgart • Moscow

A DORLING KINDERSLEY BOOK

Editor Patricia Grogan **Art Editor** Lesley Betts
Project Editor Fiona Robertson
Photography Susanna Price
Production Charlotte Traill

Managing Editor Jane Yorke
Managing Art Editor Chris Scollen

Cycling consultant Tony Yorke

The biking adventurers:
Laurence Gould, Roxanna Kashfi,
Mark Smith, Amelie Sumpter

First published in Great Britain in 1996 by
Dorling Kindersley Limited,
9 Henrietta Street, London WC2E 8PS

Reprinted 1997

Visit us on the World Wide Web at
http://www.dk.com

A CIP catalogue record for this book is available from the British Library

ISBN 0-7513-5455-4

Colour reproduction by Colourscan, Singapore
Printed in Hong Kong by Wing King Tong

Contents

How to use this book

This book contains the information you need for safe cycling trips. It shows you all the skills and techniques to practise for off-road riding, and is packed full of useful hints, tips, and ideas. Enjoy your biking adventures!

Getting started

Before setting off on a cycling trip, you will need to get the right bike. Going into a bike shop can be very confusing. There are so many bikes to choose from, and so many different bike accessories. This section gives you the information you need to get started.

Find out the difference between a mountain bike and a racing bike on page 9.

Make a tool pouch on page 13 to store your tool kit in.

Look on page 15 to learn how to feather your brakes.

Make a limbo bar on page 21 to practise cycling under low obstacles.

Back to basics

Biking off-road can be much more challenging than cycling on-road. You never know when you will have to cycle over an obstacle or up a steep hill. Learning how to use your brakes and gears properly will help you to cope in any situation.

Ready for anything

Practice makes perfect. Build an obstacle course at home to practise your cycling skills. This will give you the confidence to tackle rough ground when you are out on the trail. You can also polish your skills by playing games on your bike with your friends.

Test your cycling skills on the obstacle course shown on page 22.

Make a baton on page 25 to use when playing cycle-polo.

Make a map case on page 28 to store your map in.

Learn how to make a route card and why it is useful on page 29.

Exploring new areas

Being able to find your way, or navigate, with a map and a compass will enable you to explore new areas on your bike. This section teaches you how to plan a route, work out how long it will take you, and make sure you set off in the right direction.

Planning a trip

Going on a cycling trip is probably one of the most exciting adventures you can have on your bike. Make sure you are prepared for any changes in the weather and take plenty to drink. You could also make a logbook to record your adventure.

See page 32 for how to make a cycle cover to protect your bike.

Look on page 34 for instructions on making a logbook.

Learn how to mend a puncture out on the trail on page 38.

Find out how to get a fly out of your eye on page 42.

Safe biking

You need to look after your bike with regular cleaning, oiling, and basic maintenance. A badly maintained bike could be dangerous. It is also important to know how to look after someone if they have an accident out on the trail.

Finding out more

Lots of people enjoy cycling off-road and there are plenty of clubs you can join. However, it is important to respect the countryside and look after it so that others can enjoy it as much as cyclists do. Make sure you learn the basic rules for trail-riding.

Use the glossary on page 46 to look up useful biking terms.

The index on page 48 shows you where to find everything in this book.

How to use each page

Each double-page in this book explains everything you need to know about one subject. The introduction gives you an overview, and the step-by-step instructions show you how to learn, make, and do all the activities.

★ **Star symbol**
This symbol draws your attention to important safety points.

◉ **Wheel symbol**
You will see a wheel symbol next to every useful hint, tip, or additional piece of information.

The coloured band on each page reminds you which section you are in. This page is in the Planning a trip *section.*

Step-by-step instructions show you how to make and do everything in stages.

Locator picture
This picture sums up what is being covered on the double-page.

Materials box
Most pages have a materials box. Look here to find out the materials you will need for each project or activity.

Page name
The top right-hand corner of each page has the name of the double-page. This will help you find the correct page when flicking through the book.

Hints and tips
Each hints and tips box is full of useful information.

Hints and tips boxes have a picture of a boy or a girl. Most pages have one of these boxes.

Boxed pictures
The instructions underneath these pictures give you details on how to make and do the activities.

Extra information
At the bottom of several right-hand pages, you will find additional or new information about the subject.

When buying a bike, choose a shop with a good selection.

Which bike?

There are lots of different kinds of cycling adventure you can have and lots of different cycles to choose from, too. When you first start cycling, you do not need to get a specialist bike, but you do need to make sure that it fits you and is suitable for the adventures you want to have.

The main features of a bike

All bikes have certain features in common. Study the bike shown below to learn the names of all the different parts. This will help you to understand how your bike works and what to ask for if you need to buy spare parts.

The saddle can be covered in leather or material.

The seat post allows you to adjust the saddle height.

The pannier rack is attached to the bike at the seat stay and rear drop out.

Pannier rack

Saddle frame

Seat post

Fitting to adjust the seat post.

Rear reflector

Seat stay

Seat tube

Wheel reflector

Water bottle carrier

Rear drop out

Front mech

Tyre

The tyre has a beaded edge that grips on to the wheel.

Chain guard

Bottom bracket

Wheel rim

Chainring

The valve is used to let air in and out of the inner tube.

Sprockets

Chain

Rear mech

Chain stay

This bike has a derailleur gear system. The chain is shifted from one sprocket or chainring to the next.

Where to store your bike

If finding somewhere to store your bike at home is a problem, you could buy a cycle hook. Ask an adult to attach this hook on to a wall. You can then hang up your bike by the front wheel to keep it out of the way.

There are several kinds of gear shifter, including thumb, under-bar, and twist shifters.

Bearings contain small metal balls that enable parts of your bike to move smoothly.

Most modern bikes have quick release levers, which allow you to adjust parts of your bike very easily.

The differences between three common bikes

A mountain bike has a sturdy frame and tyres with a good grip for riding on rough ground.

A racing bike is built for speed, so it has a very light frame and large, narrow wheels.

A shopper bike is designed for riding on-road. It is often fitted with a basket.

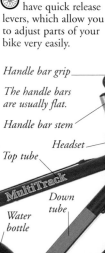

Gear shifter

Brake lever

The headset attaches the front forks to the cycle frame with bearings for smooth steering.

Handle bar grip

The handle bars are usually flat.

Handle bar stem

Headset

Top tube

MultiTrack

Down tube

Water bottle

Brake cable

Front reflector

Brake block

Front fork

Cycle pump

Pedal

Crank

Toe clip

The spokes support the wheel rim.

The quick release lever attaches the wheel to the bike.

The hubs on the front and rear wheels contain bearings and hold the spokes.

Wheel reflector

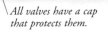

Spoke

The pedals have an uneven surface for extra grip.

Bikes with several gears usually have one, two, or three chainrings.

All valves have a cap that protects them.

You will need to use a spanner to release your wheels if they do not have quick release levers.

Whether you are riding on- or off-road, always wear a cycling helmet.

All kitted out

Being safe and comfortable on your bike can make all the difference between an enjoyable ride and a miserable one. Your most important accessory is a well-fitting helmet to protect your head. This is the only specialized item you really need. Follow the guidelines below for choosing the rest of your kit.

Your second skin

Choose clothing that is close-fitting so that there is no material to get caught up in the moving parts of your bike, but ensure it is not so tight you cannot move easily. Also, avoid trousers with bulky seams in the seat area.

Choose a helmet that has been safety-tested and is labelled accordingly.

A bandanna will help to keep you cool in the summer and warm in the winter.

Wear several thin layers of clothes so that you can remove or add layers if you get too hot or cold.

Wear a sweatshirt on cool days.

Avoid V-neck tops as they do not keep your chest warm.

Always wear or pack a wind- and water-proof jacket.

A cotton T-shirt will keep you cool in the summer.

Wear a vest under your top to absorb sweat when you are cycling.

Jogging bottoms or leggings will keep you warm on cool days.

If you plan to go out cycling for a long time, you will be more comfortable in cycling shorts than normal shorts.

Shorts are ideal for warm days.

Make sure your jacket is not too loose, otherwise it will flap about when you cycle.

Ideally, your jacket should have air vents to allow sweat to evaporate.

Cotton or wool socks will stop your feet getting too cold.

Wear shoes with a firm sole so that the balls of your feet do not get sore when pedalling your bike.

How to make sure your helmet fits you correctly

Put the helmet on and fasten the straps. Ensure it fits snugly and does not slide about.

If the chin strap is too loose, your helmet will not stay in place when you cycle over rough ground.

When adjusting your straps, ensure both sides are adjusted equally.

The helmet should sit low over your forehead to protect it, but should not obscure your vision.

Specialist clothing

Of all the specialist clothing available, cycling shorts and shoes are the most useful items for general cycling.

Choose a cycling helmet that has comfortable straps.

A water bottle that fits on to your bike is the best way to carry drinks.

Wear a top that will keep your lower back covered when you lean forwards on your bike.

The seat of cycling shorts is padded for extra comfort.

Cycling shorts fit very snugly and do not have any uncomfortable seams.

Cycling shoes have an extra-firm sole.

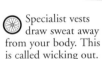

⊛ Specialist vests draw sweat away from your body. This is called wicking out.

⊛ Cycling shoes designed for racing have a clip on the sole that fastens to the pedal.

How a bandanna can help to keep you warm or cool

To absorb sweat, fold the bandanna in a triangle and wrap it around your neck.

The triangular part of the bandanna should cover the back of your neck to protect it from sunburn.

In cold weather, keep your head warm by wearing the bandanna under your helmet.

With the bandanna still folded, place it over your head and tie it at the nape of your neck.

Protecting your head and hands

Your head, eyes, and hands are most at risk from injury when cycling. A helmet is essential, and glasses and gloves are very useful.

The slits provide the ventilation.

Short-fingered mitts give you the most control.

Most helmets are made of polystyrene.

Eye protection
Goggles will protect your eyes from insects, mud, dust, and sunlight.

Cycling helmet
Look for a lightweight helmet that has good ventilation.

The adjustable padding makes the helmet more comfortable.

Cycling mitts
Wear cycling mitts to protect your hands from blisters.

Make sure your bike is properly equipped every time you go out.

Equipping your bike

Having chosen your kit, it is important to ensure your bike is also kitted out. A basic tool kit is essential – you never know when you may need to perform a simple repair. If you plan to ride at dawn or dusk, you will also need to ensure your bike is fitted with lights and reflectors so that you can be seen easily.

Materials for the tool pouch

Needle Thread

Scissors

Toe-clip straps

Oblong of material

Your essential tool kit

The items shown here will enable you to carry out basic repairs on your bike. If your bike needs any major work, take it to a cycle shop to be repaired.

Multi-purpose oil

Keep a can of oil at home so that you can oil your bike after every wash.

— Cycle pump

Choose a good quality pump that you can clip on to your cycle frame.

Screw driver

Spanner

This multi-headed spanner will ensure that you have the correct sized spanner for most repairs.

Make sure your screwdriver is the correct size for the screws on your bike.

See page 13 for the contents of a puncture repair kit.

Hints and tips

Bungee straps and toe-clip straps are very useful for securing items to your bike.

Fit a white light at the front of your bike and a red light at the back.

Measure your tools so that you know what size to make each section of your tool pouch.

Use plastic tyre levers as they are light to carry.

— Tyre lever

There are several kinds of inner tube, so check at a bike shop which kind you will need for your bike.

Inner tube

Always take a spare inner tube with you in case you get a puncture.

Tyre levers will help you remove the tyre from the wheel when you are repairing a puncture.

Spoke key

A spoke key is used to tighten and adjust the spokes on your bike.

Chain rivet extractor

— Allen keys come in several sizes.

— A set of Allen keys, like the one shown here, is ideal as you will be sure to have the correct-sized key for most jobs.

A chain rivet extractor is used to mend a broken chain.

It is difficult to mend a broken chain, so ask an adult to help you.

How to make a tool pouch to store your tool kit in

Hem the oblong of material then fold it so that the back section is larger than the front.

Sew the sides of the material together to make a pouch. Now divide the pouch into sections.

Sew straight lines through the material to secure the sections and slide the tools inside.

Fold the top of the tool pouch over and then roll the pouch up. Secure it with a toe-clip strap.

Bike accessories

Bike shops stock all the accessories you need for your bike. Some of the more important ones are shown here.

Bike computer

Some cycle bells have a simple compass that can help you tell direction.

Bell

Water bottle and carrier

Front light

Reflective arm bands

Back light

Reflective trouser clips

Reflective stickers

All new bikes are fitted with reflectors.

Reflective body strap

Bicycle lock and keys

Bungee straps

Toe-clip straps

Avoid over-stretching a bungee strap as it could spring back on you.

Pannier rack

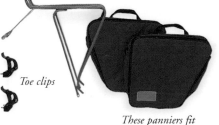

Toe clips

See page 33 for how to assemble a pannier rack.

These panniers fit over the back wheel.

How to attach your tool pouch to the bottom of your saddle

Thread the toe-clip strap around the underside of the saddle frame to make a loop.

Slide the rolled tool pouch approximately half-way through the looped toe-clip strap.

Pull the toe-clip strap tight to secure the tool pouch to the underside of the saddle frame.

When cycling over rough ground, use two toe-clip straps to make the tool pouch extra-secure.

Container for puncture repair kit

Puncture repair kit

The most common repair you are likely to undertake is mending a puncture. You can buy puncture repair kits from all cycle shops. Make sure it contains the items shown here.

See page 38 for how to repair a puncture.

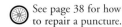

Large patches

Sand paper

Wax crayon

Chalk

Rubber solution

Small circular patches

Getting ready to ride

Before you set off on your bike, you need to ensure it fits you correctly and that every part of your bike is working properly. As long as the frame is the correct size, you can adjust the other parts of your bike to make it comfortable. Ask an adult to help you do this and carry out the pre-ride checks listed below.

When sitting on your bike, the tips of your toes should just touch the floor.

Preparing your bike

If your bike is not the correct size, it will be very difficult to ride and could even be dangerous. Equally, it is important to check that all the parts of your bike are working properly.

What size?

You should be able to stand astride your bike with both feet on the ground. When sitting on the saddle, you should be able to reach your handle bars easily while looking ahead.

See page 41 for how to adjust your handle bars.

Adjusting the angle of the handle bars may make it easier to reach the brake levers.

Remember to re-check your saddle height every few months because you are still growing.

Pre-ride checks

Always check your brakes, tyres, lights, and reflectors before every ride, and once a month, give the other parts of your bike a thorough check.

Ask an adult to help you check your tyres by squeezing in the sides.

How to adjust the angle and height of your saddle

Bikes can have Allen key or spanner fittings, or quick release levers to hold the seat post in place.

Loosen the fitting and adjust the seat post to the correct height. Now tighten the fitting again.

To adjust the seat angle, loosen the fitting under the seat with an Allen key or spanner. When the seat is horizontal, tighten the fitting again.

See page 40 for how to check the other parts of your bike.

Hints and tips

The sides of your tyres should be very firm. If you can push them in, they need to be pumped up.

All seat posts have a safety line marked on them to indicate the maximum point to which you can move the saddle up.

Make sure the pedals on your bike have a good grip for your shoes.

The correct foot position without and with toe clips

Place the ball of your foot on the pedal and push your foot down to start pedalling.

Avoid placing the heel of your foot on the pedal as your foot could easily slip off the pedal.

Flick the pedal up with your foot to lift the toe clip and then slide your foot forwards into the clip.

A toe clip will help keep your foot in the correct position and make it easier to cycle up steep hills.

When you first start using toe clips, use shallow ones without straps so that you can remove your feet easily.

With experience, you can learn to feather your brakes. Feathering is when you make rapid gentle pulls on your brake levers.

Ready to go

Now you are ready to learn basic cycling skills. Make sure you are sitting squarely on the saddle. Lean forwards slightly and keep your back straight.

Always look behind you to check it is clear before you start cycling.

Lean forwards from the hips.

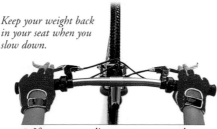

Start off by pushing the ball of one foot firmly down on the pedal.

Practise starting off with each foot forward so that you can start cycling from any position.

Keep your hands and arms relaxed.

1 For normal cycling, ensure you can hold the handle bars with your arms slightly bent. Your hands should be shoulder-width apart.

Brake lever

Brake cable

Pull the brake levers towards you when you brake.

2 Check that you can pull on both brake levers comfortably. You may find it easier to keep your fingertips on the levers all the time.

Keep your weight back in your seat when you slow down.

3 If you are cycling over very rough ground, keep two fingers on each hand over the brakes, so you are ready to brake quickly.

How the brake blocks make your bike slow down

The cable that runs from each brake lever operates the two rubber pads called brake blocks.

Pull gently on the brake levers. The front edges of the brake blocks should touch the wheel rim first.

When the brakes are fully on, the whole edge of each brake block will touch the wheel rim.

An empty car park is a good place to practise your cycling skills.

Starting out

When you first start cycling, choose a quiet place to practise. Once you feel comfortable stopping, starting, and cycling in a straight line, try turning corners. This will develop your steering skills, and is also good practise for using your brakes. After this, you will be ready to learn how to use your gears.

Materials for the cones

Coloured tape

Scissors

Coloured card

Hints and tips

Use a low gear to cycle around the cones slowly and a medium gear to cycle around them quickly.

Aim to turn each pedal around 80–90 times a minute. This is called your pedal cadence.

To work out how many gears your bike has, multiply the number of chainrings by the number of sprockets.

When cycling slowly, slightly ease off the pressure on the pedals when you change gear.

Slalom cycling

Steering is one of the most important cycling skills. Slalom cycling is being able to steer in and out of cones at varying speeds. It will enable you to cycle around all kinds of obstacle off-road.

1 Make six cones, as shown on the right. Place the cones about 2 m (6 ½ ft) apart in a zigzag shape. Now practise cycling in and out of the cones at varying speeds.

Approach each turn slowly to start with.

Practise with your friends.

Lean into the turn from your hips.

Use your brakes to control your speed.

If you feel your balance going, put one foot down.

Turn the handle bars as smoothly as you can.

2 When you can do this comfortably, move the cones closer together. You will have to steer more carefully to get around the obstacles.

Try cycling around the cones quickly. You will find that the faster you cycle, the more you will have to lean into your turns.

How to make cones to practise cycling around corners

Roll one piece of oblong card diagonally to make a cone shape. Make sure it has quite a wide base.

Tape the cone together along the long edge. You may need a friend to hold the cone for you.

Trim the card around the bottom edge so that the cone stands fairly upright.

Decorate the cone with the coloured tape. You could wrap it around the cone diagonally.

How to turn sharply to avoid unexpected obstacles

Place a cone on the ground and cycle towards it quite quickly, but still under control.

When you are about 2 m (6 ½ ft) from the cone, turn the handle bars very quickly towards it.

Immediately turn the handle bars in the direction you want to go around the obstacle.

By turning the handle bars in the opposite direction first, you can make a much sharper turn when cycling quickly.

Getting to know your gears

The gears on your bike will help you to turn your pedals at the same speed whether you are cycling slowly along a narrow path or quickly down a steep hill.

Practise feeling your gear changes rather than looking down at the gear shifter.

When changing gear, keep pedalling otherwise the chain may jam.

Gear shifter

Seven sprockets   *Chain*   *Large, middle, and small chainring*

Two kinds of gear shifter on the handle bars

If your bike has a twist shifter, you will change gear by twisting the handle bar grip.

A thumb shifter has a small lever that you push or pull to go up and down the gears.

The parts of your gear system

Most cycles have a derailleur gear system. If the bike has 21 gears, it will have three chainrings, seven sprockets, and one chain. The chain runs around one of the chainrings and one of the sprockets, depending on which gear you are in.

The front mech moves the chain across the chainrings.

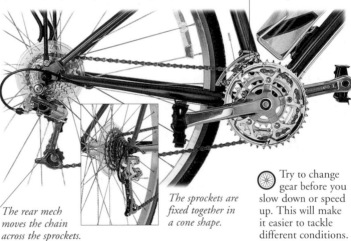

The rear mech moves the chain across the sprockets.

The sprockets are fixed together in a cone shape.

Try to change gear before you slow down or speed up. This will make it easier to tackle different conditions.

Low gears
When you use the small chainring and two or three of your largest sprockets, you are in a low gear. You will need a low gear when you are cycling slowly and climbing up steep hills.

Middle gears
You will use the middle gears most of the time. They allow you to cycle quite quickly without too much effort. Use the middle chainring with any sprocket.

High gears
When you are cycling very quickly, use the high gears. You will need the large chainring and two or three of the smallest sprockets.

Cycling across a slope requires very good balancing skills.

Up and down the trail

Whether you are cycling along a narrow path or speeding down a steep hill, you must keep your bike under control at all times. Most accidents happen when cyclists are racing out of control down steeps hills, so it is very important to learn how to use your brakes and gears effectively.

Materials for the chicane

Flower pots

Canes about 2 m (6 ½ ft) long

Making a chicane

A chicane is a narrow path that requires good balancing skills to cycle through. Follow the instructions below to make this simple chicane.

Put one end of the cane on the inside edge of the flower pot.

1 Place four flower pots in an oblong shape that is about 50 cm (1 ½ ft) wide and 2 m (6 ½ ft) long. Balance one cane on top of two of the flower pots.

Use a cane to measure the width of the chicane.

Keep the two lines of canes at an equal distance throughout the chicane.

2 Balance a second cane on the other two flower pots. Add two more flower pots about 2 m (6 ½ ft) farther along and balance two more canes in exactly the same way. Repeat this process until the chicane is approximately 6 m (20 ft) long.

Hints and tips

As a general rule, the steeper the hill, the lower the gear you will need to cycle up it.

When doing an emergency stop off-road, pull on your back brake slightly harder than your front brake.

Pull on your front brake slightly harder than your back brake when performing an emergency stop on-road.

3 Practise cycling through the chicane. Approach it slowly in a low gear. Push down firmly on the pedals and use the brakes to control your speed. Try to keep upright and avoid leaning to one side as this will unbalance you.

Sit squarely on the saddle.

The narrower the chicane, the harder it is to cycle through.

Try cycling through the chicane standing on your pedals.

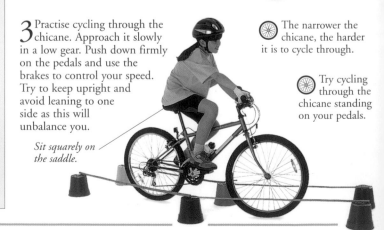

Cycling uphill

On gentle slopes, you can sit or stand while cycling, but on steep hills, you should try to remain seated all the time. This will ensure the back wheel grips the ground firmly, otherwise it could spin out of control.

To cycle up a gentle slope, keep your weight far back in the saddle and pedal with your heels down.

Grip the handle bars firmly.

On steep hills, keep your weight in the centre of the bike. Bend your arms, and bring your head forwards to stop the front wheel lifting up.

⊛ Change into a lower gear before the hill gets steeper.

Cycling downhill

You can gain a lot of speed cycling down a hill, so it is important to stay in control. Always change into a middle gear, as shown on page 17, before you go down the hill, and use the brakes to control your speed.

Grip the handle bars firmly.

⊛ Pick out a smooth path before cycling down a hill.

When cycling down a gentle slope, keep your arms straight and sit back in the saddle.

Keep your knees bent and relaxed.

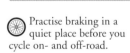

Freewheel down steep hills by keeping your pedals level. Control your speed by feathering the brakes (see page 15).

⊛ If a hill is very steep, get off your bike and walk down instead.

⊛ Practise braking in a quiet place before you cycle on- and off-road.

Emergency stops

Braking very quickly is called an emergency stop. You need to slide back on your saddle and pull gently but firmly on both brakes.

⊛ To start with, brake gently and increase the pressure on your brakes as you slow down.

If you pull too hard on your back brake, you are likely to skid. This is because your back wheel will lock and push you off-balance.

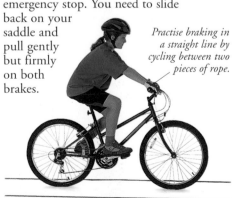

Practise braking in a straight line by cycling between two pieces of rope.

Pulling too hard on your front brake will make your bike tip forwards. In extreme cases, you could even tip forwards with it.

In some conditions, it may be more sensible to get off your bike and push it.

Coping with obstacles

Half the thrill of cycling off-road is coping with the changing conditions. You could find yourself cycling under low branches, carrying your bike over very rough ground, or even hopping over small logs. You need special skills to cope with these conditions, so learn the techniques shown here before you set off.

Materials for the cycle-limbo

Coloured tape

2 cones made on page 16

Canes 2 m (6 ½ ft) long

Log

When to carry your bike

If you come across ground that is so steep or bumpy you cannot cycle over it safely, you will need to get off your bike and carry it.

⊛ Always lift your bike from the left-hand side to avoid the greasy chainwheel and sharp sprockets on the right-hand side.

Lean the bike against you.

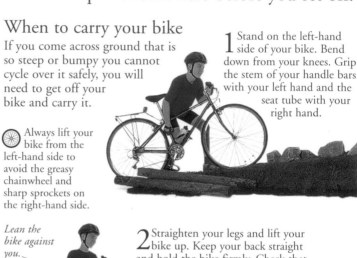

1 Stand on the left-hand side of your bike. Bend down from your knees. Grip the stem of your handle bars with your left hand and the seat tube with your right hand.

2 Straighten your legs and lift your bike up. Keep your back straight and hold the bike firmly. Check that the wheels are far enough off the ground to clear the obstacles.

⊛ If you try to cycle over very rough ground, you could damage your tyres.

Hints and tips

⊛ Use toe clips to help you pull up the pedals when you are hopping over obstacles.

⊛ If you know you will have to carry your bike, try to keep it light by not attaching extra equipment to it.

3 If you are carrying your bike over very large boulders, you may need to lift it higher. Bend your right arm up, making sure you keep your elbow close to your side.

⊛ If you knock your bike when carrying it over an obstacle, check that nothing is damaged.

Check the ground is firm before putting all your weight on it.

Hopping over logs

Tree roots and logs are some of the most common obstacles in woodland and forests. With practice, you can learn how to hop over these obstacles without getting off your bike.

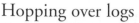

Approach the log straight on.

1 Pedal slowly towards the obstacle. Move your weight over the back of the bike and just before you reach the log, pull up the handle bars to lift the front wheel off the ground. Push the pedals downwards to give you more lift.

Use a low gear so that you have more control.

2 As soon as your front wheel has cleared the log, shift your weight forwards again. This will bring your front wheel down and get you in position for lifting your back wheel over the log.

Keep your weight over the front wheel.

3 Lift yourself out of the saddle and pedal hard so that the back wheel lifts up off the ground. When you have cleared the obstacle, sit back in the normal riding position.

Press down on the handle bars.

Pull gently on the front brake.

Make sure the obstacle is not wider than the distance between your wheels.

Push down hard on the lower pedal.

Practise cycling over a soft obstacle like a small cardboard box to start with.

How to make a limbo bar to practise cycling under low obstacles

Tape two small pieces of cane about 30 cm (12 in) apart, at right angles to the top of one long cane.

Repeat the first step and then balance another long cane along the two taped canes.

Cycle-limbo

Cycling under a limbo bar is good practice for cycling under low branches when you are off-road.

Lean your body to one side.

Look ahead

Push your bottom back.

Ultimate limbos When the limbo bar is as low as 110 cm (3 ½ ft), you will have to come right off your saddle. This requires a lot of bike control.

Put each upright cane in a cone (made on page 16).

This cycle-limbo is about 140 cm (4 ½ ft) tall.

Approach the bar slowly and freewheel under it.

Use your arms to help you keep your balance when you lean to one side.

On your obstacle course

Competing on an obstacle course is an ideal way to test your cycling skills – it is a lot harder to tackle a series of obstacles than a single obstacle. The obstacle course shown here will test a wide variety of the skills needed for on- and off-road cycling.

Cycling clubs regularly set up obstacle courses to test cycling skills.

Building your course

Pages 16–21 show you how to make all the sections of this course. Put the sections together as shown here.

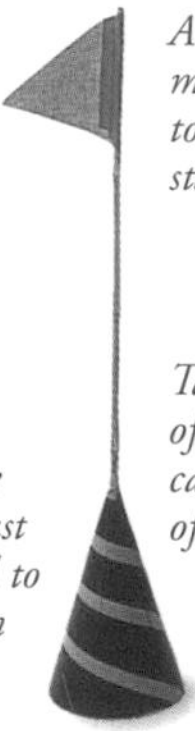

Adapt the cones made on page 16 to make two starting posts.

Tape a triangle of material or card to the top of the cane.

Approach the cones with just enough speed to stop you from wobbling.

1 Position the cones made on page 16 in a curve. You will need to cycle in and out of the cones, so make sure you space them out enough – about 2 m (6 ½ ft) apart.

Take it in turns to start.

Make sure you do not cycle too close to the person in front of you.

Ask a friend to time you with a stop watch to see how long it takes you to complete the course.

2 Place the chicane made on page 18 after the cones. To start with, make the chicane approximately 1 m (3 ft) wide. As you gain more experience, make the chicane narrower.

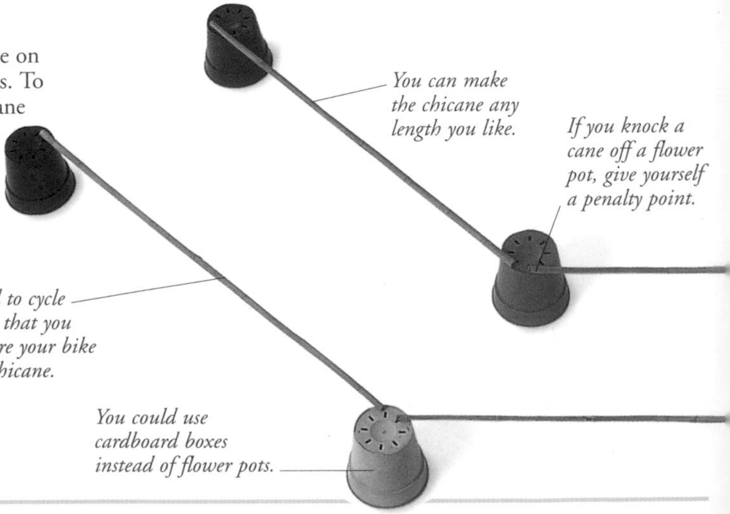

You can make the chicane any length you like.

If you knock a cane off a flower pot, give yourself a penalty point.

You will need to cycle very slowly so that you can manoeuvre your bike through the chicane.

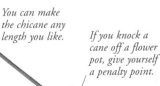

You could use cardboard boxes instead of flower pots.

Some of the skills
you will need for
cycling on a trail

Use the skills you learned
cycling under the limbo
bar to cycle under low
branches off-road.

If the ground is rough
and uneven, it is often
easier to get off your bike
and push or carry it.

Use the skills you learned
on the slalom to cycle
around pot holes,
boulders, and stones.

Cycling through the
chicane is good practice
for cycling along a
narrow path.

7 Finish your obstacle
course in style by making
two finishing posts in exactly
the same way as you made
the starting posts.

*Make this obstacle
harder by lowering
the bar.*

6 Make the limbo bar shown
on page 21 and put it at
the end of your obstacle
course. Make it quite high to
start with and lower the bar
as you gain more confidence.

5 Lay down two logs approximately
2 m (6 ½ ft) apart. Carry your bike
over the logs as shown on page 20.
When you get more experienced,
practise hopping over the logs,
as shown on page 21.

As you gain more
experience, move the
cones closer together so
that you have to turn in
between them more sharply.

*The faster you cycle around
each cone, the more you will
have to lean into the turn.*

4 Position two more cones after
the chicane. Cycle around
these cones one-handed. This is
good practice for when you are
cycling on roads and need
to give hand signals.

*Use your brakes
to control your
speed around the
obstacles.*

*This section
requires a lot of
balancing skill.*

3 When the chicane is only 50 cm (1 ½ ft) wide,
you will not be able to turn the pedals in a
complete circle. Get the pedals level and then
push each one forwards and backwards about
one quarter of a turn. Repeat this process
to move through the chicane.

*As you manoeuvre around
the first cone, be careful not
to knock the chicane with
your back wheel.*

Weaving in and out of cones is one of the most popular cycling games.

Fun and games

When you are cycling in a group, it is important to be considerate towards the other cyclists. The games shown on these pages are not only great fun to play, they are also a good way to practise cycling with other people in different conditions. Choose a safe place on the trail or at home to play these games.

Materials for the games

Tape

Flower pots

Soft ball

Rope

Scissors

Newspaper

Hints and tips

Keep your bike in a low gear to help you cycle slowly.

Make sure each team member has a turn cycling with the ball.

Always keep your distance from the other competitors.

Cycle-relay

You need two teams, with at least two people in each team, to play cycle-relay.

Place flower pots at either end of each rope to mark the start and finish lines.

1 Lay three lengths of rope in straight lines 1 m (3 ft) apart. One person in each team starts at one end of the rope lanes with a soft ball and cycles to the other end.

2 A second person from each team waits at the other end of the rope lanes to collect the ball from the first team member.

Pass the ball to the second team member.

Be ready to start cycling as soon as you have the ball.

Make sure each team member has a turn cycling with the ball.

3 The second team member then cycles back to the other end of the rope lanes with the ball. The first person across the finish line wins for his or her team.

Slow race

As its name suggests, this race is all about how slowly you can cycle. The last person to cross the finish line is the winner.

Standing up on your pedals may help you balance more easily.

Balance is the key to winning this game.

Use two pieces of rope to mark the start and finish lines.

Finish line

If you cross the finish line before the others, you lose the game.

If you put your foot down, you are out of the game.

Feather your brakes to help slow you down.

Cycle-polo

Whether you are having a drink while cycling on the track, or indicating to turn on the road, you will need to cycle one-handed at some point. Cycle-polo is a fun game to play that will help you to practise cycling one-handed.

Practise using alternate hands to bat with.

1 Position several plant pots about 2 m (6 ½ ft) apart in a zigzag shape. Make a baton, as shown on the left, and get a soft ball.

Weave in and out of the flower pots.

How to make a baton with newspaper for playing cycle-polo

Ask a friend to time how long it takes you to complete the course.

2 The aim of the game is to bat the ball around the flower pots. Take it in turns to start, and leave at least 5 m (16 ft) between each cyclist.

Hit the ball very gently so that you have more control.

Take approximately five sheets of newspaper and roll them lengthways to make a long tube.

You will need to practise turning your handle bars with just one hand.

3 Always bat the ball ahead of you around the flower pot and then cycle slowly after it. As you gain more experience, you can try cycling quickly around the obstacles.

Use your brakes to control your speed.

Secure the tube by wrapping pieces of coloured tape around it at 10-cm (4-in) intervals.

25

How to read a map

If you want to explore new areas on your bike, you should always take a map with you, so you do not get lost. Maps show you the exact position of objects and what the land, or terrain, is like. Study all the features on the map shown here so that you can learn how to read a map of your area.

Learn how to read a map so that you can explore new places.

Legend

▬▬▬	Major road
══════	Minor road
= = = = = = =	Track
●	Town
)(	Bridge
───────	Railway line
▬	Railway station
▲	Woodland
⬭	Lake
∿∿	River
⅄	Marshland
─100─	Contour line

Land-height bands
0–100 m
100–200 m
200–300 m
Over 300 m

The north point shows you where north is on the map.

The legend tells you what all the symbols on a map represent.

⊛ Maps often use slightly different symbols to represent the same objects, or features. Study the legend on your map carefully so that you know what each symbol represents.

The land height is shown as blocks of colour on this map. This allows you to see changes in land height at a glance.

When there are a lot of woodland symbols close together, the wood is very thick.

⊛ Study this map carefully and see if you can work out an interesting route to cycle along. Try to avoid major roads.

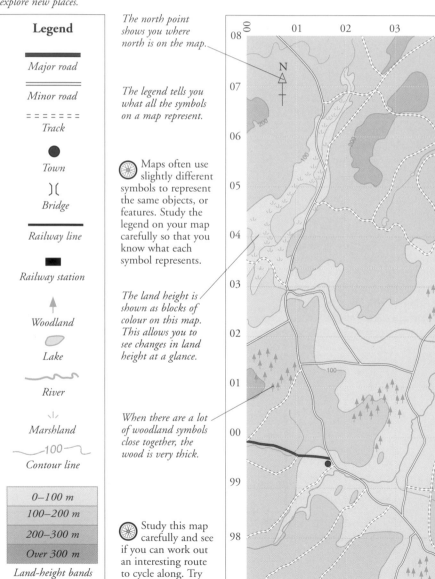

Understanding contours

One of the most noticeable differences between a map and the land it describes is that a map is flat, but the land is bumpy. Contours solve this problem. A contour line is an imaginary line that follows the ground surface at a specific level. When the contour line is drawn on the map the land height appears next to it. You can then look at a series of contour lines to work out where the ground changes height.

How contour lines are measured and drawn on a map

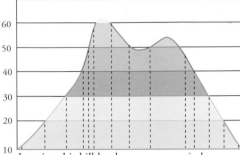

Imagine this hill has been cut across in layers every 10 m (33 ft). Draw an imaginary line around the edge of each layer.

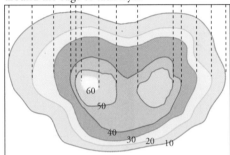

When these imaginary lines are placed together on a map, they form contour lines. Follow the contour lines to work out the shape of the hill.

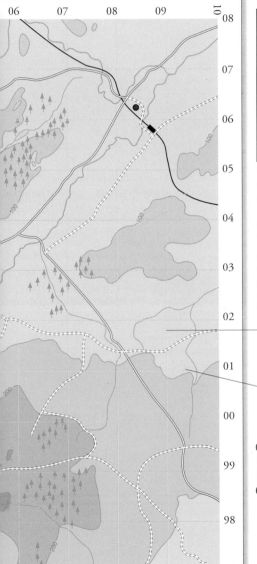

Most maps have a grid of squares on them. The lines are drawn at regular intervals and are numbered so that you can refer to any point on the map by giving these numbers.

The grid lines that run down the map are called eastings.

The grid lines that run across the map are called northings.

If contour lines are close together on the map, the changes in land height are very steep. If they are widely spaced, the change is much more gradual.

When you give a grid reference, write down the easting number that is on the left of the point first, and then the northing that is below the point.

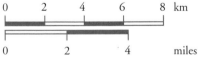

Scale bar

Everything on a map is scaled down and drawn to a fraction of its real size. On this map the scale is 1:50,000. This means that 2 cm on the map is equal to 1 km on the ground.

Always take the time to plan your route before setting off on your trip.

Choosing your route

Before setting off on any cycling trip, you need to plan your route. This is especially important if you are exploring a new area. When choosing your route, think about how long you want to go out for. If the land, or terrain, is going to be quite rough, it will take longer to cycle over than flat terrain.

How to make a map case

This map case will protect your map. You can also mark your route on the case, rather than writing on the map itself.

Materials

String

Waterproof tape

Card strip

Plastic sleeves

Scissors

1 Seal the sides of two plastic sleeves, as shown on the right. Now, join the sleeves together on one side by taping the open end of one sleeve to the short, closed end of the other sleeve.

2 Strengthen the corners of the plastic sleeves, as shown on the right. With a pair of scissors carefully make one hole in each corner of the joined sleeves.

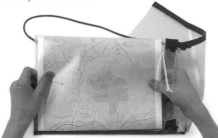

3 Make a carrying strap, as shown on the right. The bottom sleeve will form the map case. Fold your map so that it fits into the case and you can see the area you plan to cycle through.

More details on how to make a map case with plastic sleeves

Wrap a strip of waterproof tape along the long open side of the plastic sleeve to seal it.

Fold the sleeves over so the top sleeve is open at the bottom. Tape the top corners for extra strength.

Thread a piece of string through the holes to make a loop to hang the case around your neck.

The card will become your route card. Slide it in to the top sleeve. Fold the sleeve and tape it shut.

Hints and tips

Leave a copy of your route and the time you expect to arrive back with an adult. If you get lost or are late back, he or she will know where to look for you.

Make a plastic sleeve by folding a sheet of plastic in half. Tape one long and one short side.

Which way?

Once you know how long you want your trip to last, choose a place you would like to get to, for example a hilltop with a good view. Now, work out the best way to get there and back. Try to avoid major roads and look for interesting tracks to follow instead.

Use a water soluble pen or crayon to draw your planned route on the plastic map case.

1 Decide where you will start your route. If you are arriving by car, you will need to start your route near a road. Choose a point that is close to a track so that you will not have to cycle along the road for long. Now work out a route along the tracks that will lead you to the hilltop.

If you are going along the same section of a track twice, draw a symbol to remind you, otherwise you may get confused later.

2 Try to make your route circular so that you are not doubling back on yourself. On this route, we have gone down the hill and then followed a track that goes around the other side of the hill back to the starting point.

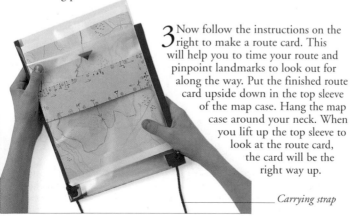

3 Now follow the instructions on the right to make a route card. This will help you to time your route and pinpoint landmarks to look out for along the way. Put the finished route card upside down in the top sleeve of the map case. Hang the map case around your neck. When you lift up the top sleeve to look at the route card, the card will be the right way up.

Carrying strap

How to make a route card to help you follow your route

Take the card out of the sleeve and put one corner on your start point. Draw a symbol to represent it.

Pivot the card so it aligns with the route. Mark on the card the point at which the path bends.

Continue pivoting and aligning the card with your route. Draw a symbol for each point.

Follow the route all the way around the card. Draw arrows to remind you of the direction.

Align the finished route card with the scale bar on your map. Divide the route up into one-kilometre sections.

See page 30 to find out how and why you may need to shorten your route.

Navigating on your bike

You never know what is going to happen on your trip, so always be prepared. Make sure you can shorten your route if you get tired or the weather changes. Also, learn how to use a map and compass together so that you can check you are going in the right direction. This skill is called navigation.

Check your map and route card often to ensure you do not get lost.

Planning escape routes

Study your route carefully and try to work out where you may get tired. If you plan to cycle up several hills, it is a good idea to make sure you have a number of escape routes near the hills. An escape route is another route you could follow to shorten your trip. If you think the conditions may change, choose several escape routes so you can shorten your trip at any time. Study the escape routes shown on the map below.

You also need to think carefully about your rest stops. Try to choose places that either give you a good view, provide shelter, or are interesting.

Examples of interesting places to stop for a rest

A bridge is often a good place to rest. It is an obvious landmark to use when checking your map.

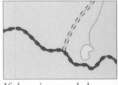

If there is a pond along your route, try to have a rest stop next to it so that you can study the wildlife.

Cycling to the top of a hill is very challenging, and it also provides an excellent view.

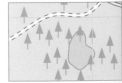

A wooded area will provide shade, which is very appealing on a hot summer's day.

The red lines represent the planned routes.

The green lines represent the escape routes.

If your escape route takes you along a road, make sure you know the road rules for that area.

This escape route may not look very short but it is on flat ground, so will be quick to cycle along.

Choose an escape route near your lunch stop. If you find you are tired after lunch, you can then go home.

More details on how to use a map and compass to navigate

The edge of the compass should align with your starting point and the first section of the route.

Make sure that the arrow on the ruler section of the compass is pointing in the direction you want to go.

The needle that moves around when you move your compass always points north.

Having checked your direction, follow the trail marked on the map.

Finding your way

If you are cycling in a new area, use your map and compass to check you are going in the right direction.

1 Place your compass on your map over your starting point (see the detailed instructions on the left). Keep the map flat.

Practise using a compass before you set off on a trip.

2 Turn the dial on your compass around until the red arrow on the dial runs parallel with the upright, or vertical, grid lines, on the map.

3 Keep the compass firmly on the map and turn the map around until the needle that moves (see the detailed instructions on the left) sits on top of the arrow on the compass dial. You are now facing north. Look at the arrow on the ruler section of the compass. It is pointing in the direction you need to go.

Hints and tips

A compass has a magnet in it, so make sure you do not put it near anything made of metal. If you do, it will not work properly.

When the map is pointing north, the writing and symbols will be the right way up.

If you are cycling on a windy day, aim to cycle into the wind on the way out. By doing this, you will have the wind behind you on the way home.

What is a bike computer?

A bike computer is a very useful accessory. It fits on your bike and gives you a lot of information about how you are cycling.

You can use a computer to tell you how fast you are travelling, how far you have gone, and your average speed.

Bike computers are usually waterproof, so you can keep them on your bike all the time.

Most computers add up how many kilometres or miles you have cycled since you attached the computer to your bike.

The computer attaches to the handle bars of your bike. A cable runs from the computer down to a sensor on the front wheel. It measures how many times a minute the wheel is turning, and how quickly.

Most computers tell you the time, so you do not need to wear a watch.

Push the buttons on the computer to use the different functions.

Practise cycling with a loaded bike before you set off on an expedition.

Preparing for your trip

Having chosen your route, you need to pack your kit. Only pack what you really need, as an over-loaded bike is difficult to ride. It is also important to be prepared for changes in the weather. The cycle cover shown below will keep you dry if it rains and can also double-up as a picnic sheet in sunny weather.

Materials for the cycle cover

String   Tape

Stapler

Pebbles

Scissors

Plastic sheet

Hints and tips

Remember to take your map, route card, and compass with you on your trip.

Pannier racks are either assembled with an Allen key or a spanner.

Make sure that both pannier bags weigh the same. If they do not, you will find it difficult to balance.

Put heavy items at the bottom of the panniers.

Making a cycle cover

This cycle cover is very quick to make and light to carry, so take it with you on all of your trips.

1 Lean your bike against a solid object, such as a tree trunk. Tie your bike to the trunk by wrapping a piece of string or a bungee strap around the trunk and the seat post of your bike.

Short side of sheet

2 Get the plastic sheet and cut it into an oblong 3 m x 2 m (10 ft x 6 ½ ft). Pull one of the short sides up over the front of your bike.

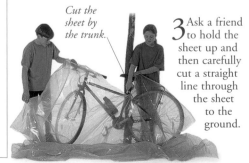

Cut the sheet by the trunk.

3 Ask a friend to hold the sheet up and then carefully cut a straight line through the sheet to the ground.

More details on how to make a cycle cover with a sheet of plastic

To make the cycle cover completely watertight, secure all the folds with a piece of tape.

Staple the taped folds for extra strength and then put a second piece of tape over the top of the staple.

Pull out the bottom of the cycle cover by wrapping a pebble in each corner of the plastic.

Hold the pebble in place by tying a piece of string around it. Keep one end of the string long.

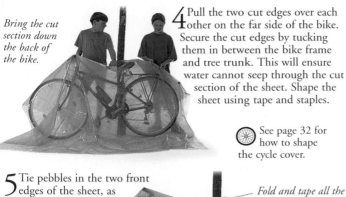

Bring the cut section down the back of the bike.

4 Pull the two cut edges over each other on the far side of the bike. Secure the cut edges by tucking them in between the bike frame and tree trunk. This will ensure water cannot seep through the cut section of the sheet. Shape the sheet using tape and staples.

See page 32 for how to shape the cycle cover.

See page 32 for how to shape the cycle cover.

5 Tie pebbles in the two front edges of the sheet, as shown on page 32. Pull the edges out and tie the long ends of the string to two secure objects.

Fold and tape all the parts of the cover that touch your bike.

Leave a gap between the sheet and ground to let air in.

Tie the string to another tree trunk.

Packing for your trip

Whether your trip is going to last one hour or a whole day, you will need to take provisions with you. If you are going on a short trip, take a drink, waterproof top, tool kit, and first aid kit with you. For longer trips, include the items shown here in your pannier bags.

Record your trips in a logbook.

Always take a first aid kit with you and learn how to use it.

Choose high-energy food that is easy to carry for your lunch. Sandwiches, crisps, and fruit are ideal.

Pack sunglasses if it is likely to be a sunny day.

Take toe-clip straps to secure loose items on your bike.

Take a pair of warm trousers, such as jogging bottoms, in case it gets cold.

A bandanna will help to keep you cool in the summer and warm in the winter.

Pack a spare pair of socks. If your feet get cold, you can put the socks over your shoes.

These pannier bags clip on to the sides of a pannier rack.

If you plan to cycle at dawn or dusk, pack reflective bands. Wear them whenever the light is poor.

Be prepared for changes in the weather by packing a waterproof top.

How to attach a pannier rack to your rear wheel

Screw all the parts of the rack together following the manufacturer's instructions.

Screw the bottom of the pannier rack to the hole on the rear drop out. Do not tighten the screw yet.

Lever the pannier rack over the wheel so that the flat top of the rack sits over the top of the wheel.

Attach the front "arms" of the rack to the seat stay. Tighten the screws at the seat stay and rear drop out.

The panniers will hang down the sides of the rack, so you can attach extra items to the top.

Some pannier bags are joined together. The join sits over the top of the pannier rack.

Recording your trip

Having gone to all the effort of planning your route and preparing for your trip, it is a good idea to keep a record of it in a logbook. Your logbook can contain lots of information, including where, when, and who went on a trip. It can also have a diary section for noting special things you do and see along the way.

Always try to make room for your logbook in your panniers.

Materials for the logbook & pocket

Scissors ||| *Crayons*

String

Sheets of paper

Small piece of plastic

Plastic sheet

Pen

Needle

Thread

Material

Hints and tips

Sew a back pocket on your T-shirt to store items you use a lot. This will save you getting off your bike and hunting through your panniers.

Hemming the material on your pocket will stop the edges fraying.

Making a logbook

Make this logbook at home following the instructions below.

1 Cut the plastic sheet to size, fold the sheets of paper in half, and pierce holes in the paper and plastic as shown on the right.

2 Put the folded paper on the plastic, making sure all the holes line up. Thread a piece of string through the holes as shown on the right.

Tie a bow in the string on the outside of your logbook.

The plastic sheet makes your logbook waterproof.

3 The basic logbook is now completed. Follow the instructions on page 35 to add a pocket to store your pens in.

More details on how to make a logbook

Cut the plastic sheet so that it is about 2 cm (1 in) wider all around than the sheets of paper.

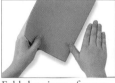

Fold the pieces of paper in half and press down firmly along the edge to make a crease.

Carefully pierce two holes in the folded section of the paper. Ask an adult to help you.

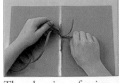

Thread a piece of string through the holes in the folded paper and then through the plastic.

How to make a pocket to store pens in the logbook

Tape the small piece of plastic to the top sheet of paper. Remember to leave the top open!

Make sure that the pocket is deep and wide enough for your pens and crayons.

Fold over the long edges of the plastic cover and tape them down to keep the logbook closed.

Remember to have plenty to drink on your trip.

Filling in your logbook

It is entirely up to you what you put in your logbook. Here are some examples of items you could record.

1 Stick a photograph of you and your friends in your logbook. Make a note underneath it of your planned route and the date. This will mark the starting point of your trip.

2 Keep a record of what you see along your route. You could press leaves in your logbook, record the wildlife, and stick down postcards of places you have visited.

3 When you stop for a rest on your trip, make notes in your logbook. You can record where you stopped for lunch, what the weather was like, if you found the route tiring – anything you think is interesting.

When you take a break, look at the map to check where you are going next.

How to make a pocket on a T-shirt to store extra items

Cut an oblong of material that is almost the width of your T-shirt. Hem the edges of the material.

Sew the hemmed material to the back of your T-shirt. Leave the top edge open.

Make two pockets by sewing a line up the middle of the material and the T-shirt.

Store soft items in your pocket, such as your mitts, bandanna, and any snacks.

Sit on the cycle cover you made on page 32.

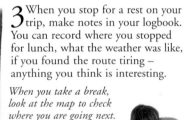

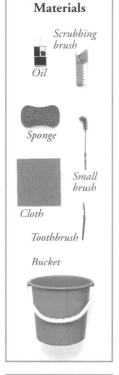

You must clean and oil your bike after every muddy ride.

Bike cleaning and oiling

It is amazing how much dirt can cling to your bike when you are cycling off-road. Cleaning and oiling your bike regularly will stop the dirt from building up and will also make it run better. You should give your bike a wash after every muddy ride and a thorough clean several times a year.

Materials

Scrubbing brush

Oil

Sponge

Small brush

Cloth

Toothbrush

Bucket

Cleaning your bike

Turn your bike upside down so that you do not have to lean it against anything. Fill a bucket with warm soapy water and wash the whole bike, paying particular attention to the areas shown below.

You could rest your saddle on a cloth so that you do not scratch it.

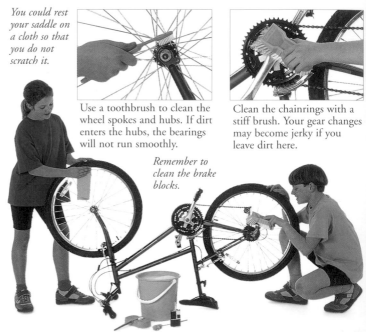

Use a toothbrush to clean the wheel spokes and hubs. If dirt enters the hubs, the bearings will not run smoothly.

Clean the chainrings with a stiff brush. Your gear changes may become jerky if you leave dirt here.

Remember to clean the brake blocks.

Store all your cleaning materials together.

Hints and tips

You can use a hose pipe to wash off most of the mud if you are careful not to spray any of the moving parts.

Avoid using a vegetable-based oil for oiling your bike as it leaves a sticky residue.

Use a soft sponge and plenty of soapy water to clean the frame. This will ensure you do not scratch the paintwork.

Remember to rinse the soapy water off your bike.

Use a small brush to clean the sprockets. Be very careful when doing this because the sprockets are quite sharp.

Oiling your bike

After you have given your bike a thorough clean, you will need to replace the oil you have washed off. This will ensure that all the moving parts of your bike work smoothly and do not rust. Turn your bike the right way up for oiling, otherwise the oil will drip down on to your handle bars and saddle.

Oil the moving parts of the brakes. If you spill any oil on the brake blocks, clean it off thoroughly with soapy water.

If the paintwork is scratched, touch it up with some paint. This will help to stop your bike going rusty.

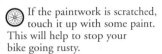

Oil the chain in sections. Push the pedal backwards to move the chain around, so you can oil a new section.

If you get oil on the brake blocks, they will not work properly.

Check the quick release levers and other fittings on your bike are properly secured.

Push the arm of the rear mech down so that you can oil the jockey wheel – the two small wheels in the rear mech.

Keep a look out for any parts on your bike that need adjusting or repairing.

Oil the moving parts of the front and rear mechs. Check which parts move by asking a friend to turn the gear levers.

Always make sure your bike is completely dry before you start oiling it. Otherwise, the oil may not reach the bearings and the other moving parts.

QR levers

Quick release levers are often called QR levers for short. These fittings are very popular on bike wheels and saddles as you do not need any tools to undo them. However, if you do not close a lever correctly, it could be dangerous.

The correct position
When the lever is closed correctly, it will curve inwards towards the wheel.

The incorrect position
If the lever curves outwards, it is open and not locked, making your bike unsafe to ride.

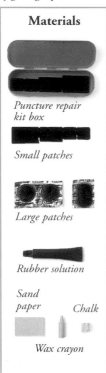

Cycling over rough
ground runs the risk
of getting a puncture.

Repairing a puncture

Each wheel has an inner tube full of air. If
you get a puncture, you will have to replace
or repair this tube. Repairing an inner tube
can take a while, so take a spare one out with
you. Then, if you do get a puncture, you can
replace the inner tube with your spare tube,
and repair the damaged one at home.

Materials

Puncture repair
kit box

Small patches

Large patches

Rubber solution

Sand
paper   Chalk

Wax crayon

Hints and tips

You will also
need your basic
tool kit to repair a
puncture. Page 12
shows you what you
need in your tool kit.

Removing a rear
wheel is quite
complicated, so ask
an adult to help
you if the puncture
is here.

Changing tubes

The instructions below
show you how to replace
an inner tube.

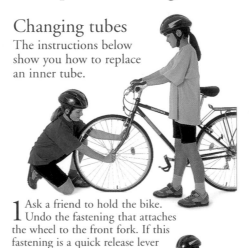

1 Ask a friend to hold the bike.
Undo the fastening that attaches
the wheel to the front fork. If this
fastening is a quick release lever
(see page 37), you just need
to open the lever.

Lean the tyre
against you
to keep it
still.

2 Slide one
tyre lever in between the tyre and wheel rim.
Repeat with a second tyre lever a little farther
around the wheel. Push down on the tyre levers
to prize one side of the tyre off the wheel rim.

Leave one side
of the tyre on
the wheel.

3 Release any air
left in the inner
tube through the
valve, as shown
on the right,
and pull the
inner tube out.

More details on
how to replace an
inner tube

Unclip the brake cable
from the brake block so
that you can slide the
wheel out more easily.

If your wheels are not
attached to your bike by
quick release levers, you
will need to use a spanner.

Schrader valves are found
on mountain bikes. To
release the air, push down
on the valve pin.

Racing bikes have presta
valves. Release the air by
unscrewing the top and
pushing in the valve pin.

More details on how to replace an inner tube (continued)

Feel along the inside of the tyre to find out what caused the puncture, and remove it.

Push the tyre over the top of the wheel rim so that it slots back into place and holds the inner tube in.

Check the inner tube is covered by the tyre and is not pinched between the tyre and wheel rim.

To find the hole in a damaged inner tube, pump a little air into it and immerse the tube in some water. Air bubbles will come out of the hole.

Remember to take the punctured inner tube home with you.

Hold the tyre in between your legs to keep it upright.

Pump a little air into the spare inner tube to help prevent it catching between the tyre and wheel rim.

4 Push the inner tube valve into its hole in the wheel rim. Slide the new inner tube between the tyre and wheel rim. Push the tyre back in place, as shown on the left.

Ask a friend to hold the wheel steady.

Make sure your bike pump has the correct fitting for the valves on your bike.

5 Pump up the tube and check that it is not bulging off the rim anywhere. If it is, stop pumping and straighten the inner tube before continuing.

6 You are now ready to put the wheel back on the bike. Slide the wheel between the front fork and brake blocks and secure the wheel to the front fork. Clip the brake cables back on the brake blocks. Check your brakes still work properly.

See page 37 for how to check your quick release levers are in the correct position.

How to repair a damaged inner tube with a puncture repair kit

Use the wax crayon to draw a circle around the hole in the inner tube, so you can see it easily.

Sand the smooth surface of the inner tube around the hole with the sand paper to make it rough.

Spread a small amount of rubber solution around the hole. Leave it to dry for five minutes.

Remove the foil backing from a patch and stick it over the hole. Leave it to dry for five more minutes.

Peel off the Cellophane covering. Sprinkle chalk dust over the patch to soak up any extra glue.

The underside of the puncture repair kit box has a special surface to rub chalk over to make chalk dust.

Maintaining your bike

Cycling off-road causes a lot of wear and tear on your bike, and if you do not look after all the parts, they will wear out very quickly. By carrying out the basic maintenance checks shown on these pages, the parts of your bike will last longer and you could save on expensive repairs.

Keep your tools together in a tool pouch, so you can find them easily.

Checking the cranks

The cranks hold your pedals in place. They are quite low to the ground and can work loose when cycling over rough ground. Check the cranks regularly – if you cycle with a loose crank it could become damaged. To test your cranks, grip each crank and and try to rock it from side to side.

Hints and tips

Clean your tools with an old rag each time you use them.

If you are unsure which tool to use for a specific job, ask at your local cycle shop.

Whenever you take anything apart, always lay out the separate pieces in the order they came off the bike.

When you tighten a crank, remember to hold the pedal securely with one hand.

The chainwheel bolts keep your chainwheel in place.

Never use a screwdriver in an Allen key fitting because you will damage the hexagonal hole.

Tightening the cranks

If there is a dust cap covering the crank fixing, remove it and put it in a safe place. Check to see which kind of fixing your cranks have and follow the instructions below to tighten them.

1 Cranks fixed with a sunken nut need a special spanner that fits into the recess. Turn the spanner clockwise to tighten the nut.

2 To tighten a crank with an Allen key fitting, use the correct-sized Allen key (usually 8 mm) and turn it clockwise.

Use an Allen key to check the chainring bolts are not loose.

You may need adult help to ensure the cranks are tight enough.

How to recognize a worn brake cable and brake block

Check the brake cables regularly for signs of fraying. If you find any, the cable needs replacing.

This brake block has worn down so much that it will not work effectively.

Adjusting your handle bars

Before you set off on a ride, you need to know how to adjust the height and angle of your handle bars so that you can adapt your bike to fit you properly. It is also important to check that the stem is securely tightened. Put the front wheel between your knees and try to twist the handle bars. If the stem moves, the bolt needs tightening.

How to adjust the height and angle of the handle bars

Loosen the stem bolt and raise or lower the stem to the correct height before tightening the bolt again.

Loosen the stem clamp to rotate the handle bars. Remember to tighten the stem clamp afterwards.

⊛ The stem clamp is at the front of the handle bars.

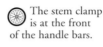

Stem bolt

Stem

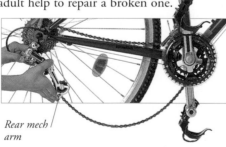

Grip the front wheel between your legs to steady the bike.

⊛ The stem bolt and clamp are loosened with a spanner or an Allen key.

⊛ The stem should have a saftey line marked on it. You can move the handle bars safely up to this maximum point.

⊛ The rear mech and chainring are quite far apart, so ask a friend to help you.

How to release the tension in the chain

Push the arm of the rear mech forwards. This will push the chain forwards and make it hang loosely.

When you turn the pedal backwards, keep the chain pulled away from the chainring.

Unjamming a chain

If your chain gets jammed, you must release it immediately, otherwise the chain could break. It should be easy to release a jammed chain, but you will need adult help to repair a broken one.

Rear mech arm

2 Hold the chain and turn the pedal backwards slowly until the chain has moved all the way around the chainring and rear mech. This will release the jammed chain. Release the arm of the rear mech so it pulls the chain tight again.

⊛ Turn the pedals backwards when releasing the chain, as this will not push the back wheel around. If you push the pedals forwards, the wheel will turn too.

1 Before you can find the cause of the jammed chain, you will need to release the tension in the chain (see the instructions on the left).

Keep your first aid kit waterproof by packing it in a plastic bag.

Materials

Triangular bandage to tie arm slings.

Scissors to cut plasters.

Plasters of varying sizes

Safety pins for securing slings.

Gauze pad for treating cuts and grazes.

Antiseptic cream to clean cuts and grazes.

First aid

No matter how carefully you cycle, accidents can still happen. The very nature of cycling means that you will usually be away from home when an accident occurs, so always take a first aid kit with you. The techniques shown on these pages show you how to deal with the most common cycling injuries.

An object in your eye

If you get a fly or piece of grit in your eye when you are cycling, you will soon feel it. Your eye will water and feel sore. Ask a friend to help you remove the foreign body.

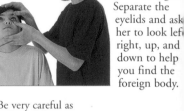

Tilt her head back

1 Sit the patient down, facing towards the light. Separate the eyelids and ask her to look left, right, up, and down to help you find the foreign body.

★ Be very careful as the surface of the eye is very delicate.

Use clean gauze or a triangular bandage to remove the foreign body.

Aim for the inner corner of her eye.

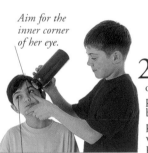

2 If you can see the foreign body, wash it out with water. Ask the patient to tilt her head back and then pour plenty of clean water over her eye.

Ask the patient to look away from the water.

3 If the foreign body does not wash out, carefully lift it off the eye with a clean, damp piece of cloth.

4 Sometimes you will not be able to see the foreign body, for example when it is under the eyelid. In these cases, ask the patient to lift her upper eyelid slightly outwards and then downwards over the lower eyelid. This should clear away the foreign body.

Hints and tips

If you cannot remove the foreign body from your patient's eye, get adult help immediately.

⚙ Put round-ended scissors in your first aid kit. If you use scissors with sharp ends, they could make a hole in the plastic bag.

How to tie an arm sling with a triangular bandage

Place the bandage between the patient's bent injured arm and chest. Bring one end up around the neck.

Bring the lower end of the bandage up over the front of the forearm to the end at the shoulder.

Tie the two ends together just below the shoulder. Pin the loose fabric to the bandage with a safety pin.

Use an arm sling to support an injured elbow, lower arm, or wrist.

Take care not to prick the patient with the safety pin.

How to tie an elevation sling

If the patient has hurt his or her collar bone or shoulder, you will need to support the arm on the injured side with an elevation sling.

1 Bring the arm on the injured side up and across the patient's body. Ask her to support her elbow with her other hand. Get a clean triangular bandage from your first aid kit.

Support the arm on the injured side.

Hold the top corner at the shoulder.

2 Lay the triangular bandage over the injured arm. Make sure the top of the long edge is hanging on the uninjured side so that when you secure the bandage, the knot sits on this side.

3 Fold the bottom of the long edge under the injured arm. Scoop the bandage under the elbow and around the back of the patient.

4 Bring the long edge of the bandage diagonally across the patient's back and up to the far shoulder. Make sure the elbow is held securely in the fabric.

5 Tie the two ends of the bandage just in front of the shoulder on the uninjured side. Gather the loose fabric and secure it with a safety pin.

If you do not have a safety pin, twist the loose fabric and tuck it inside the sling at the elbow.

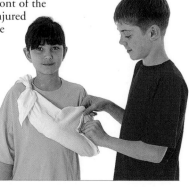

How to treat cuts and grazes with a clean gauze pad

Gently wash the injured area with clean water. Use a clean gauze pad or very soft brush.

Try to wash off any bits of dirt or gravel. Be very gentle, as this may cause some fresh bleeding.

Get a clean pad, gauze is ideal, and apply pressure to the injured area to stop it bleeding.

Stick a plaster over the injured area, making sure it has a pad large enough to cover the wound.

Rules for the trail

To make sure that all your cycle trips are enjoyable and safe, it is important to follow a few golden rules. When cycling in a group, always follow the instructions given by the leader. Respect the countryside you are travelling through, and be considerate of other people and animals along your route.

Be considerate on the trail so others can enjoy safe rides after you.

When you reach the top of a hill, take time to enjoy the view with your friends before cycling down again.

If the trail is wide and smooth, you can cycle two abreast. However, if the trail is narrow or rough, or you are cycling around obstacles or up and down hills, cycle in single file. When you cycle up a hill, keep your distance from the other cyclists and wait at the top for the rest of your group before cycling down the hill.

In good cycling conditions, keep a cycle-length's gap from the rider in front.

The leader should ensure you have regular rest stops.

Most serious accidents happen when cyclists go too fast downhill. Keep your distance from the cyclist in front and feather your brakes to keep your speed under control. This will reduce the risk of skidding.

Even if you are cycling along a straight and smooth path, there are still certain guidelines you need to follow. One experienced cyclist should lead the group and a second experienced cyclist should stay at the back of the group to make sure no one is getting too tired or is left behind. Aim to cycle with people who have a similar amount of cycling experience as you.

If the group is not cycling fast enough for you, ask the leader if you can cycle ahead for a few minutes and then double back to the group. This will allow you to cycle faster and farther while still staying close to the group.

Countryside Code for cyclists

Always follow the Countryside Code when you are out on tracks and trails. This will ensure that the countryside remains a place that everyone can enjoy. The points shown on these pages are especially important for cyclists, so make sure you learn them before you set off.

 Some trails are not open to cyclists. Always check that you are allowed to cycle along a track or trail before you do so.

Take your empty drinks cans and other rubbish home with you. Do not litter the countryside because you could harm wildlife.

Do not light fires – they can easily get out of control.

Leave gates as you found them – either open or closed. If a gate has been left open, there is almost certainly a reason for it, such as cattle being moved to another field.

Keep to cycle trails and never ride through fields because you may damage crops.

Be considerate towards all animals you meet on the trail. If you scare them, they could injure you or themselves.

Give way to any walkers you meet on the trail. Get off your bike if the path is narrow.

Do not pick flowers or pull up plants. It is very destructive, and in some places it is even illegal. Take photographs and do drawings to record what you have seen instead.

Avoid a track if it goes along an unfenced water's edge. If you end up on one and the path is narrow, get off your bike and push it until you reach a safer trail.

Wear brightly-coloured clothes so that you can be seen easily. This is very important on dull days.

Glossary

Allen key
A six-sided, L-shaped tool used to adjust an Allen bolt. Bike gears and brakes often have an Allen key fitting.

Bearing
Found in the wheel hub, pedals, headset, and bottom bracket. The bearings contain small balls that enable the moving parts to work smoothly.

Bike computer
A small device that is attached to your handle bars and front wheel. It measures how quickly you are cycling, your average speed, how far you have

travelled, and tells you the time. Some bike computers can even tell you your pedal cadence.

Bottom bracket
The bracket that joins the seat tube to the down tube and houses the crank bearing.

Brake blocks
The two rubber

pads that touch the wheel rim to slow down the bike when the brake levers are pulled.

Chicane
A very narrow path that requires good balancing skills to

cycle through. *It is pronounced shecane.*

Crank
The arm that joins one pedal to the bottom bracket and gear system.

Derailleur gear
A popular gear system found on many bikes. It works by moving the bike chain from one sprocket or chainring to the next.

Dust cap
A protective covering found on an inner tube valve and on the crank fixing.

Feathering
A way of braking by pulling the brakes on and off several

times in quick succession. This kind of braking reduces the risk of skidding when cycling downhill.

Freewheel
To cycle without pedalling. This technique is used for coasting down hills.

Front mech
The part of the derailleur gear system that is fixed to the seat tube. It moves the chain from one chainring to another, and is also called the front derailleur.

Headset
The fitting that attaches the front forks to the cycle frame. The headset has bearings for smooth steering.

Hub
The centre of a wheel that contains bearings and an axle around which the wheel turns.

Jockey wheels
The two small wheels found in the arm of the rear mech. They are used to guide the chain.

Logbook
A diary for

recording the details of your trip.

Navigation
How to find your way, usually with a map and compass.

Pannier bag
A bag that can be attached to the front or rear wheel of a bike. A pair of pannier bags hangs from a rack either side of the front or back wheel.

Pedal cadence
The speed at which the pedals are pushed around. The ideal pedal cadence is about 90 turns a minute.

Quick release lever
Also known as a QR lever, it is a fitting used to hold the wheels and saddle in place. QR levers are found on most modern cycles.

Rear mech
The part of the derailleur gear system

fixed to the right-hand rear drop out. It moves the chain from one sprocket to another, and is also called the rear derailleur.

Slalom
A race that requires skill to cycle around a series of objects. *It is pronounced slarlom.*

Spoke
A thin rod that runs from the hub to the rim.

Stem
The tube that attaches the handle bars to the headset.

Toe clip
A device attached to a pedal. It is designed to keep your foot in the right place on the pedal.

Toe-in
The angle at which a brake block touches the wheel rim.

Tyre lever
A plastic or metal lever that is used to prize the tyre from the wheel rim.

Valve
The device on an inner tube through which you can pump or release air.

Wicking out
The ability of a specialist fabric to draw sweat away from your body.

Useful organizations

British Cycling Federation
(including mountain biking)
National Cycling Centre
Stuart Street
Manchester M11 4DQ

Federation of Irish Cyclists
Kellyroche House
619 North Circular Road
Dublin 1
Republic of Ireland

Scottish Cyclists' Union
The Velodrome
Meadowbank Stadium
London Road
Edinburgh EH7 6AD

Welsh Cycling Union
3 Sandown House
Dalton Road
Port Talbot
West-Glamorgan SA12 6SH

Cyclists' Touring Club
Cotterell House
69 Meadrow
Godalming
Surrey GU7 3HS

British Cyclo-cross Association
14 Deneside Road
Darlington
County Durham DL3 9HZ

The English Schools Cycling Association
21 Bedhampton Road
North End
Portsmouth PO2 7JX

Countryside Commission
John Dower House
Crescent Place
Cheltenham
Gloucestershire GL50 3RA

Youth Hostel Association
(England & Wales)
Trevelyan House
8 St Stephen's Hill
St Albans
Hertfordshire AL1 2DY

Irish Youth Hostel Association
61 Mountjoy Street
Dublin 7
61 Sraid Moinseo
Baile Atha Cliath 7

Scottish Youth Hostel Association Offices
National Office
7 Glebe Crescent
Stirling FK8 2JA

Index

Acknowledgments

Dorling Kindersley would like to thank:

Trek UK for supplying the bikes, Dr Rachel
Carroll and Dr Simon Carroll for advice on first
aid procedures, and Stan Turner, Senior Coach,
at Lee Valley Cycle Circuit.
Cartography: David Roberts, Jane Voss
Illustrations: Nick Hewetson
Picture research: Sharon Southren
Picture credits: T top; B bottom; C centre;
L left; R right; A above

J. Allan Cash Photo Library: 23 TL, CL, CLB, 26T,
45CLA, CA, CB, CRA, CRB, BL; Allsport UK Ltd
Pascal Rondeau: 36T; Anton Want: 22T; Robert
Harding Picture Library/Ian Tomlinson
Photography: 44T; Images Colour Library: 20T,
23CLA; Pendle Engineering, Nelson, Lancashire:
9TL; Raleigh Industries: 9CR; Stockfile/Steven
Behr: 8T, 10T, 16T, 24T, 28T, 30T, 38T, 44C, BR,
BL; 45TR, CLB, BR; Zefa Pictures Allstock: 32T